web smart

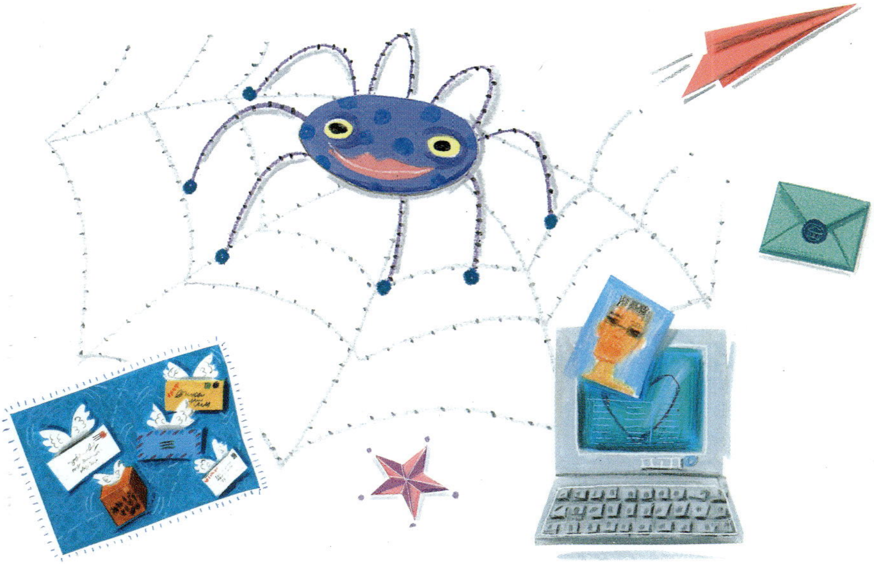

Anne Rooney
Illustrated by Debi Ani

First published in the UK in 2001 by
Big Fish, an imprint of C&B Children's Books,
London House, Great Eastern Wharf,
Parkgate Road, London SW11 4NQ
www.bigfishonline.co.uk

Copyright © Big Fish 2001

All rights reserved. No part of this book may be
reproduced or utilized in any form or by any means,
electronic or mechanical, including photocopying,
recording or by any information storage and retrieval
system, without permission in writing from the
publisher except by a reviewer who may quote brief
passages in a review.

ISBN 1903174 589

British Library Cataloguing-in-Publication Data for this
book is available from the British Library

Printed in China

Project Management: Honor Head
Project Editors: Paul Dowswell,
    Kate Phelps
Designer: Angela Ashton
Illustrator: Debi Ani

CONTENTS

Get connected	4
First stop	10
Search me!	16
What can I do?	24
What can I get?	32
Time to talk?	40
... or prefer to write?	46
Smart browsing	56
Useful words	62
Index	64

GET CONNECTED

You've got a computer and the world has got a Web – how do you get your computer to be a part of it? If you're new to this lark, start here to find out.

LEARN TO...

- find what you're going to need
- get started
- pick a name and password for yourself

If you've already got an Internet connection, go straight to the next chapter.

What a tangle

The Internet is a big, tangled network of computers spanning the whole world. It uses the phone network to let computers 'talk' to each other. You can hook into it if you connect your computer up to the phone line in your house. And once you're there, you can wander around the World Wide Web, send e-mails and chat to your friends with text messages.

What to get

To get started, you're going to need the following...

A modem: this is a bit of equipment that connects your computer to the phone line. It converts information from your computer into a form that can be carried along the phone lines. Then it brings information from the Internet into your computer, changing it back to a form your computer can understand. It might be a box that sits on the desk, or it might be a card inside your  computer. If you don't have a modem already, find out all you can about your computer before you go out to buy one. For example, you'll need to know whether you have a Mac or a PC and what version of Windows your computer is using if it is a PC.

A phone socket: you plug your modem into this. You can use this socket for a phone, too, if you have a special socket doubler. Your modem doesn't need to be plugged in when you aren't using the Internet, but it doesn't matter if you leave it plugged in. It won't stop you getting phone calls and it won't cost anything, except when you're actually using the Internet.

An account with an Internet Service Provider (or ISP):
this is a company that gets you on to the Internet. Your computer uses the modem and phone line to connect to the ISP's computer and from there you can get to all the goodies on the Internet. You can find CD-ROMs which will get you hooked up to ISPs in computer magazines and in many supermarkets and book shops. The CD installs the software you need to get to the ISP's computer and use the Internet. Make sure you get PC software if you have a PC or Mac software if you have a Mac.

A web browser: this is a bit of software that lets you use the World Wide Web. If you already have one on your computer it's likely to be either Internet Explorer or Netscape Communicator (also called Navigator). If you haven't, there will be a web browser on the CD you get from your ISP.

Your computer: you don't need the latest model of computer, but you need one that will work with your modem and run a web browser. So not your dad's antique Amstrad from the 80s or your Nintendo!

> Computers aren't the only things you can use on the Internet these days. You might be able to use your cable TV or even your phone.

Out of touch

When you go on to the Internet your phone line is in use, so you won't be able to get any phone calls and no one will be able to use a phone on the same line to make any calls. It's best to check that it's OK for you to use the Internet before you start. Remember that someone is paying the phone bill, too (unless you get free calls to your ISP). It's usually charged at the same rate as a local call, but it can mount up if you spend hours surfing.

GEEK-SPEAK

When you're connected to the Internet, you're 'on-line'. When you're clicking around from one web page to another, you're 'surfing' or 'browsing'. For more geeky words, check out the 'Useful words' on page 62.

Your ISP

Run the software from your ISP and it should set up everything you need. You'll just need to follow the instructions and make a few choices.

You'll have to give some details (like your name and address) and choose a name and password to use on the Internet. The name you choose will probably be used for your e-mail address too, along with the @ (say 'at') symbol and the name of the ISP (such as Yahoo or AOL).

You won't be able to have a name someone else has already chosen, so your chances of being just 'jo@…' or 'ahmed@…' are around zero, but if your name's Tendayi, Lucrezia or Isambard you might be in luck. You could be able to use both your first and second names together, or an unusual nickname. You'd then get an e-mail address like this:

- mirandacoburn@myisp.com
- slicknick@myisp.com
- jayne_edwards3@myisp.com

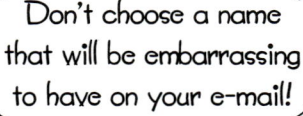

Don't choose a name that will be embarrassing to have on your e-mail!

Friend or foe?

You'll need a password, too. This is so that only you can log in (that's geek-speak for get to and use your account) as yourself. Choose a password you will be able to remember but that other people using the computer won't be able to guess.

HELP BOX

When you type your password in, it appears as a row of dots or stars, like this: ✶✶✶✶✶✶

That's so that anyone looking over your shoulder can't see what you typed – it doesn't mean your computer has gone wrong.

When you're setting up your account, you will probably be asked if you want the computer to remember the name and password you chose so that you don't need to type them in each time you go on-line.

HELP BOX

Safety first

You've probably heard about nasty stuff on the Internet. But remember that you don't have to look at anything you don't like. If you follow a link to somewhere horrid, just go back again.

FIRST STOP

If you've got all the kit and the software, you're ready to go!

LEARN TO...

- start up and use a web browser
- check out the home pages of websites including the Whizz Kids website
- follow links between pages
- go back through the links you've followed
- get back to where you started from

Ready for take-off

When you're ready to launch yourself into cyberspace, make sure your modem's plugged in to the phone socket and turned on and then start up your web browser. There might be a shortcut to it on the desktop. It will be an icon (little picture) something like this:

Internet Explorer   **Netscape Communicator**

The icon might be found on the desktop's background or it might be on a button on a toolbar (see page 11).

If you can't find a shortcut, you can get the browser from a menu. If you're using a PC, click the 'Start' button and look in the 'Programs' menu. If you're using a Mac, click on the 'Apple' menu and look around – you'll probably find it in 'Recent Applications' or 'Internet Access'.

Your computer will dial your ISP's computer and after a short while you'll see your first web page. Congratulations – you're there!

How to browse

Have a look at the browser window before you start. Whichever browser you're using, you'll need to know a bit about the window. Here's a window in Internet Explorer:

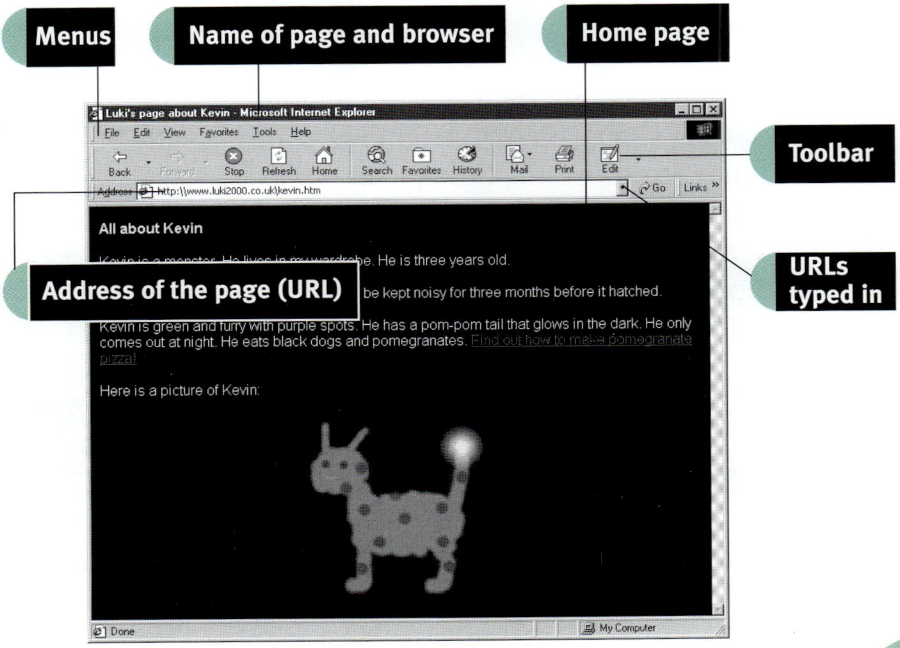

- Menus
- Name of page and browser
- Home page
- Toolbar
- Address of the page (URL)
- URLs typed in

And here's the top part of a window in Netscape:

Home from home

The first page you see is called the home page. It can be a bit confusing because two different things are called a home page:

- the page that opens when you start the browser or that appears when you click on the 'Home' button in the browser window.

- the first page in a website that has lots of pages. If you ever build your own website, the page that comes up first when someone visits your website is also a home page.

The home page that appears when you start your browser might be your ISP's page, or it might be some other page chosen by the people who made or sold the computer or by someone else who has used it. You'll find out how to change the home page to something more useful in 'What can I do?' on page 24.

Be a whizz!

Every web page has an address, or URL ('uniform resource locator' in geek-speak). This tells the computer where to ask for the page. Here's the URL of the Big Fish website:

www.	bigfishonline.	co.	uk
this bit shows it's a website on the World Wide Web	this is the name of the site	this shows it's a commercial site	this is the country it belongs to

And here's the URL of the Whizz Kids website:

www.	bigfishonline.	co.	uk/	whizzkids/	index.htm
				this is the part of the website	and this is the name of the page

You don't need to type the 'http://' and if the name of the page is 'index.htm' you don't need to type that either as the browser guesses that bit!

Follow a link

The World Wide Web is made up of more than a billion (1,000 million) web pages linked together. You can follow a link from one to another by clicking on it. A link might be:

Words that are underlined or in a different colour.

Buttons with words written on them, like 'Home' or 'Contents'.

Small pictures, or icons.

So you know you are pointing to a link, the pointer changes from an arrow to a hand.

DID YOU KNOW?

www stands for World Wide Web, but scientists are already planning to extend it to other parts of the solar system – computer stations orbiting other planets will carry web servers. In a few years, start looking out for addresses that end '.sol' – that will mean the server isn't on Earth!

Don't get lost

Now take half an hour to put your feet up and surf around and find out as much as you can on your own. Do a bit of exploring by following links to see what you can find that looks cool. If you get somewhere that doesn't have any promising links, or is boring or unpleasant, click on the button like this to go back a page:

You can use it again and again to retrace your steps to somewhere more promising.

And if you want to start again, click on the 'Home' button to go back to the home page that opens when you first go on-line.

If you want to get back to a page you've already been to, click on the arrow to the right of the address of the web page you are looking at (see page 11). A dropdown list of addresses you've typed in will appear. You can click on the right one to go back to that page.

SEARCH ME!

If you've just browsed around for half an hour, you've probably already got an idea of how much stuff there is out there. How are you going to find your way around? Start here to find out!

LEARN TO...

- find interesting websites with a directory
- use a search engine
- be a whizz with a search engine

Finding out

You won't always know exactly where you want to go. Luckily, there are lots of tools to help you find out. You can follow links from sites you've found and revisit places you like, but to find totally new places to go you'll need to use a search engine or a directory.

Directory enquiries

A directory organizes web pages into groups according to what they're about. So you'll find lists of topics like 'Sport', 'Kids', 'Science', 'News' and so on. If you want to find out something about, say, a football team, you'd click 'Sport' and then another list would appear, with different sports topics. You just keep on clicking till you get where you want.

A directory is good if you know the sort of information you want but not exactly what you're looking for. So if you want to know about new movies coming up or see the weather report for the place you're off to on holiday, a directory is a good place to start.

Have a go yourself. A directory with lots of stuff for kids is www.yahooligans.com.

Search engines

A directory is not so good if you want to know something very precise, like how to look after a rabbit, how to make an origami dragon or how many moons Jupiter has. For questions like this, you'll need a search engine. It sounds like some kind of machine but it's really just another kind of website – one that lets you search all the other millions of websites to find what you're looking for.

A good search engine is www.google.com

SPIDERS AND BOTS

Sounds horrid, but spiders and bots are the names for the bits of software that keep a search engine going. They spend their time crawling around the Web finding out what's there and making a big, big index of it all. When you ask the search engine to find something, it has an ultra-quick look through its index and shows you what it's got.

Which one to try?

There are lots of search engines to choose from. On the Whizz Kids website – **www.bigfishonline.co.uk/whizzkids** – there are links to some you might like to try out. Although they all look a bit different, they work in much the same way.

All search engines have a box for you to type the words you're looking for and a button to click to start the search. Your search engine might offer you other options, like which language the pages must be in, or how many results you want to see at once. There might be an option to build up a complicated search, which goes to a screen with even more options.

As you work through this chapter, have a go at a few search engines and choose the one you like best.

Needle in a haystack?

Searching for the one page in the billion-plus web pages that will tell you how to fix a broken furby, build a bat box or cheat at your Gameboy game might seem like looking for a needle in a haystack. But you just need to develop some basic search skills and you'll find your way through the maze.

Search 1,326,920,000 web pages

needle+haystack

You can search for a single word, but unless it's a pretty unusual word, you'll find loads of pages. More often, you'll want to search for several words together or a phrase.

If you were a frisbee freak, you might just type 'frisbee' and search for that. You'd find out what sort of frisbee websites there are, and would find some interesting links to follow.

But if you were looking for frisbee competitions to enter, you'd want to narrow down the search to get where you wanted more quickly. To do this, you need to think of two or more words to search for – called 'keywords' – that together sum up what you want. So you might look for 'frisbee competition' or 'frisbee contest'.

Linking words

Many search engines will look for sites that have both 'frisbee' and 'competition' in if you type this. But others will find sites that have either 'frisbee' or 'competition' (or both) and that won't be much use – you'll find out about different models of frisbees and competitions for the fastest cockroach to cross a table top.

Instead, you can type 'frisbee + competition' to find only sites that have both words or the phrase 'frisbee competition' in them.

So to find how to build a bat box, try 'bat+box' and if you want to fix your furby try 'furby+broken' or 'furby+fix'.

You can type 'and' instead of '+' if you like.

Turn those pages!

If the search engine finds lots of pages, there will be a button to look at the next set it's found. They are usually organized so that the most useful are listed first, but the search engine doesn't always get the list quite right.

Minus points

Sometimes, there will be words you don't want to find in your search. Imagine you wanted to find out about the constellation Orion. If you just search for Orion, you'll get pages about the Greek myth of Orion and about the car, Ford Orion. You could try 'Orion+star', but you'd still get pages that said the Orion is a 'star performer'.

But you don't have to wade through lots of car blurb: you can use '−' (minus) or 'not' to say you don't want pages about cars. You should find something useful if you try:

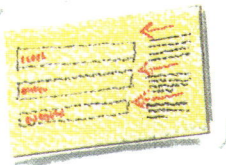

HELP BOX

Check your spelling. If you spell the words wrongly, the search engine won't find anything!

WHAT CAN I DO?

Once you're a whizz with a search engine and a directory and you know how to type in a URL, you can go anywhere – so what do you want to do?

LEARN TO...

- play games
- visit other places
- send cards to your friends
- find out about things to do away from the computer
- get help with your homework, a hobby or a tricky question
- mess about on-line!

Cool places to go

There are lots of exciting things you can do on the Internet. Check out this chapter to find cool things to do on the Web. You can even go on a virtual holiday!

Play a game

You can play on your own on-line – try games like hangman, a maze puzzle, a fishing game or a space invaders clone. Or you can play with someone else on-line, using games like chess or subuteo, racing virtual cars or building and ruling empires.

You can find trial versions of games that you can buy, then try them on-line or download them and try them out before you spend your money. (Look at the next chapter 'What can I get?' on page 32 to find out about downloading.)

Some computer games have their own sites on the Web – either somewhere to download extra goodies to go with what you've got or somewhere to swap tips and even play on-line with other people.

Check out the links to cool places where you can do these things on **www.bigfishonline.co.uk/whizzkids**

Get away!

Can't get out of school for a holiday? Go away on the Web instead! There are webcams all around the world. (Webcams are cameras that take digital stills or videos, which are posted on websites.) They show everything from scenes on a beach in Mali to the inside of a fridge (boring!). Or you can wait at a haunted site to see if a ghost pops up on-line, or peer into the crater of an active volcano (scary!). Some explorers and adventurers post pictures from their travels, so you could even go on an exciting expedition without leaving your bedroom.

Don't forget that all the time you spend on-line is adding to your phone bill!

Out of this world

If there's nowhere in the world you want to go, check out NASA's pictures from other worlds. There are webcams in space, and shots from the Hubble Space Telescope and space probes are all up on the Web if you really want to get away from it all.

...and send a postcard

You can send postcards, birthday cards or just a 'hello' card to a friend with an e-mail address. So visit the website for San Diego zoo and send your mum a postcard to tell her where you've gone.

To send a web card you need to know the e-mail address of the person you want to send it to. Pick a picture and a greeting – you can even send a moving picture and a bit of music – and wait for them to send you one back.

Enquire within

The Web's like a really, really big encyclopaedia where you can find out almost anything. You can use it to help with a hobby or your homework, or to find help on something important to you – like what to do if you're being bullied at school or if you've got a special medical condition.

You can usually find what you want using a directory or search engine, but if you're stuck there are lots of websites that are there just to answer your bizarre questions.

Real people alert

If you think you need a real, live person to answer your question, find one of the 'ask-an-expert' sites that deals with the topic you want. The expert doesn't usually sit around waiting for questions, they log on every now and then to read and answer the questions, so you probably won't get your reply immediately. And if it's a hard question, you might have to wait while they do some research or ask an even more expert expert!

Check out:
www.bigfishonline.co.uk/whizzkids
for a list of sites that might be able to answer your trickiest questions.

Off-line activities

Whatever you like to do when you're not using the computer, you can probably find out about it on the Web. If you're in a club or society – a football supporters' club or an animal charity – you'll probably find they have a website. You might be able to team up with other kids in different countries and join in with international activities.

If you play a sport, have a hobby, keep a pet or like a particular comic or TV series or movie, there's bound to be lots about it on the Web. And if you're in a band you can find out about making music on the Web and maybe even find somewhere to post samples of your own music for others to share.

If there's a cause you're passionate about, sign an on-line petition or take part in a discussion group.

Get out

If you're sick of sitting in front of the computer, take a few more minutes to find out what's on in your area – check out the cinemas, find out what's going on at the sports centre or whether any of your favourite bands are coming soon – and then go out and do it.

WEBCASTS

Visit a webcast event – that's an event, like a concert or a carnival, that is broadcast live over the Web. There's a video feed from the event to a web page. You can go to places you'd never get tickets – or transport – to in real life.

Chill out and mess about

All too serious? Then just kill time by reading on-line magazines and comics (called 'e-zines'), trekking around an on-line dinosaur museum or making a digital pizza to have delivered to your desktop!

If you don't want to read web pages, listen to web radio – radio stations that broadcast only on the Web. (You'll need speakers to be able to hear it!)

Bookmarking

When you find something you really like and you think you might want to come back to it, you can add a 'Bookmark' (if you're using Netscape) or add it to your list of 'Favorites' (if you're using Internet Explorer). Look in the 'Bookmarks' or 'Favorites' menu to find out how to add the page in the browser window to the list. To go back to it another day, just open the same menu and click on the name of the page you want.

There's no place like home

If you really, really like a page and want to make it your home page (the page that opens first), do this:

- using Internet Explorer, open the 'Tools' menu and choose 'Internet Options'. There's a button on the 'General' tab to change your home page to the one currently in the window.

- using Netscape Communicator, open the 'Edit' menu and choose 'Preferences' to set the home page.

WHAT CAN I GET?

There are loads of freebies you can get on the Web. There's also other stuff that you can pay for if you want it (and you've got a friendly grown-up with a credit card to hand).

LEARN TO...

- get free stuff on to your own computer
- find out what you can get on-line
- give back some of your own stuff

Gimme, gimme

To get something from someone else's website on to your computer, you need to download it. This just means that a copy of it is sent to your computer, where you save it on to the hard disk.

You'll need to pick where to save it and what to call it. If you download a big file (like a movie clip or a computer program) it can take a long time. Don't forget that this ties up the phone line and might cost a lot. Check it's OK to do it before you start.

Download time

Often, the page you're using gives you an idea of how large the file is or how long it will take to download. The time will depend on the speed of your modem. If you have a fairly new modem, it is probably at least 56.6 kbps. (The number shows how much information per second your modem can download. A lower number means your modem is slower and downloading will take longer.)

Take a picture

As soon as you start doing your own stuff on the computer, you're going to want to use pictures. If you're a dab hand with a painting program, you can make all your own. But for the rest of us, the Web's a mine of brilliant clip art just waiting to be snapped up and dropped into your posters, stories, invites, web pages...

GEEK-SPEAK

Clip art is the name for pictures that have already been made by someone else. You just download them from a website and use them in your own work.

Is it ok?

You can get drawings, cartoons, photos, animations and even video clips. Check what you are allowed to do with them (there will be a note on the site you take them from). Usually you can use them without asking for special permission as long as you aren't planning to sell what you've made.

Clip art formats

Clip art is usually in the form of 'gifs' or 'jpegs'. These are two different ways the computer can understand pictures. Check that the computer program you want to use them with can handle these types of file before you download lots of them. You can do this by going to the 'File' menu and choosing the 'Save as' box. There is a space at the bottom of the dialogue box labelled 'Save as type' and to the right of the file type shown is an arrow. If you click on this, a menu of different file types will drop down. The program can understand any of the types listed.

Surround sound

As well as pictures, you can find free sound files. These might be special sound effects that you can use in your own multimedia or web pages or clips of music. You can even download quite long pieces of music or whole songs.

Don't use bootleg sites – these illegally copy music for you to download for free. They cheat the people who make the music.

Free software

Software in the shops costs a lot. If you don't have much pocket money and you don't want to wait till your birthday or Christmas, hunt out some cool stuff on the Web. You can get all kinds of programs for free – either fully functional ones that people have developed for fun and are happy to share with you or demos that you try out before buying a full version.

What's the catch?

There are different types of free software, but often there's a catch. Some is genuinely free. You download it and you can use it for ever. Some is shareware. There are different deals, but often you download it for free to try out. If you decide to carry on using it, you are asked to pay a small fee.

Often, you can get a trial version of software that is for sale. It may stop working after a month or it may be only part of the package (you perhaps get only one level of a game or can't save or print work you do with a program).

The idea is that if you like it, you buy the full package – but if you don't like it, you haven't spent anything and you might have had some fun trying it out. Sounds fair.

No room for a pet? Get a cyberpet that lives in your computer! It costs nothing to feed and never messes the carpet. Check out:
www.bigfishonline.co.uk/whizzkids
for places to adopt a homeless cyberpet.

...and extras

You can often get extra bits and pieces to use with software you've already got. For example, you can download slick fonts to use with your word processing software or painting program.

You may also be able to get updates for your software that add new things to do. Check the site of the software publisher (it will be shown on the box or the CD). For games, you can often download new characters, backgrounds or game scenes.

Even if you haven't got much special software, you can download wallpaper to decorate your desktop, screensavers, pointers, sound effects and icons for your bits and pieces.

HELP BOX

If you've got virus protection software on your computer – and you should have – download updates for it to keep you in the virus-free zone.

Tell me a story

If you can't get to the library and want something to read, there are loads of books available on-line. A few you have to pay for, but there are lots (especially old ones) that you can get for free.

It's really useful if you're working on a book at school and want to include chunks in your essays – download the whole lot and copy and paste the bits you want.

HELP BOX

To copy text out of a web page, select it and then press 'Ctrl' or 'Option (⌘)' and 'C' at the same time. Click in a text document and press 'Ctrl' or 'Option' and 'V' to paste it in.

Hot gossip

You can also find stuff about the books you read off-line – sites dedicated to the stories and characters put up by the author, the publisher or by other fans. Check out the Web for juicy factoids and gossip about your favourite Harry Potter character or Jacqueline Wilson novel.

Interactive activities

If you want to do something a bit more interactive, there are loads of puzzles and colouring sheets to download. So download some Teletubbies colouring sheets to keep your baby brother or sister off your back while you search for Hogwarts-approved spells to turn them into a toad!

Give me some space!

One of the most inspiring things you can get on the Web is space – space to store or share your own stuff. Many ISPs will let you have space to put up your own web pages, and some even have tools to help you build your pages.

If you've written some stories, painted pictures or made music, there are lots of sites you can put them on to share with other people. You could even contribute to an on-line magazine or join in a story-writing group or put up some of your work in an on-line gallery.

> Check out:
> **www.bigfishonline.co.uk/whizzkids**
> for places to send your masterpieces.

TIME TO TALK?

You can talk on the phone or face to face with someone anytime, but you can also use the Internet to talk to your friends. You can keep in touch with old friends or make new ones.

LEARN TO...

- use a chat room
- send instant messages

Chat rooms

A chat room is a bit of space set aside on the Internet for you to talk to other kids. Instead of really talking, you type what you want to say and they can see what you've said as soon as you click the 'Send' button.

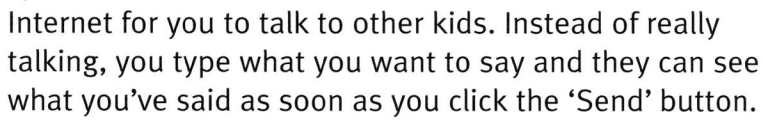

Make sure you use the special chat rooms that are set up for kids, then you won't get bored by people droning on about their mortgage problems or complaining about the government. Kids' chat rooms are moderated to make sure no grown-ups come in and make nasty suggestions, so you'll be safe there, too.

How they work

You can chat with several people at once, and they can be people you already know or new friends you've made in the chat room. It works like this:

- You find a chat service – there are links on the Whizz Kids website. You'll need to register, so pick a name you want people to use in the chat room and a password you can use when you log in to it.

- Pick a chat room that looks interesting and go right in – there will be instructions on the page.

- As each person makes a contribution, it appears on the screen for everyone else in the chat room to see. Watch for a little bit to see the sort of thing other people are saying. It's not very polite to come in and make a remark that's totally off-topic – it's like walking into a room and interrupting the conversation.

- When you've got something to say, type it in. Other people will respond to what you say, and you're in!

HELP BOX

Hanging around a chat room without saying anything is called 'lurking' and is considered rude. It's a bit like hanging around in the kitchen at a party instead of joining in. It's OK to do it for a few minutes when you've just got there, but don't stay there too long or you'll miss all the fun.

What's your game?

There are special-interest chat rooms where you can talk about anything from football to Gameboy cheats with other kids as keen as you are. Look up 'chat' on the Whizz Kids website to find out where to natter about your favourite subject.

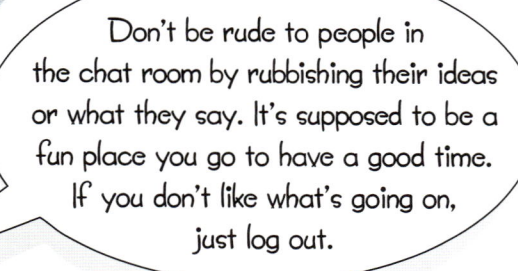

Don't be rude to people in the chat room by rubbishing their ideas or what they say. It's supposed to be a fun place you go to have a good time. If you don't like what's going on, just log out.

SERIOUS STUFF

Never give your name, address or phone number to someone you meet in a chat room, and never arrange to meet them in real life. If you want to do this – if you find you've met a nice-sounding kid from just around the corner – ask a grown-up before you do it, and never meet the person without a grown-up with you.

Remember, you can pretend to be anyone you like in a chat room, and so can everyone else. That nine-year-old who knows all about Digimon might really be an 80-year-old granny in Kansas who's never going to show at your local park however long you wait.

Old faces, new places

Half the fun of chat rooms is meeting new people. But the other is meeting up with old friends! You can arrange to meet your school friends or friends from far away in a chat room. It's better than the phone as no one else in the house can listen in. And if they aren't local friends, it's even cheaper than phoning.

Private conversation

If you don't want to go into a chat room but want to chat on your own with someone you know already, you can use instant messaging. You'll need a bit of instant messaging software, which you download from a chat service. When you go on-line you can pick the friend you want to chat to, and no one else can interrupt.

Pick the right moment

You can only send messages or chat to someone who's logged on, so work out with your pals when they want to chat. You might have a regular time – anyone who feels like it drops in between 4 and 5 in the afternoon, for instance. Or you might pick a special time when you all turn up for a bit of a party. You can all arrange to have the same popcorn or pizza at your computer desk while you gossip.

The cool thing about chat is that distance doesn't matter. Your friends in California and Australia can join in, too (as long as they're awake!).

HELP BOX

Can't work out the time difference? Arrange your meetings in Internet time. This divides the day into 1,000 'beats' of equal length and it's the same time all round the world. So 750 Internet time in Dubai is also 750 Internet time in Birmingham, Mexico City, Milan and Atlanta. The Whizz Kids website has a link to the home of Internet time.

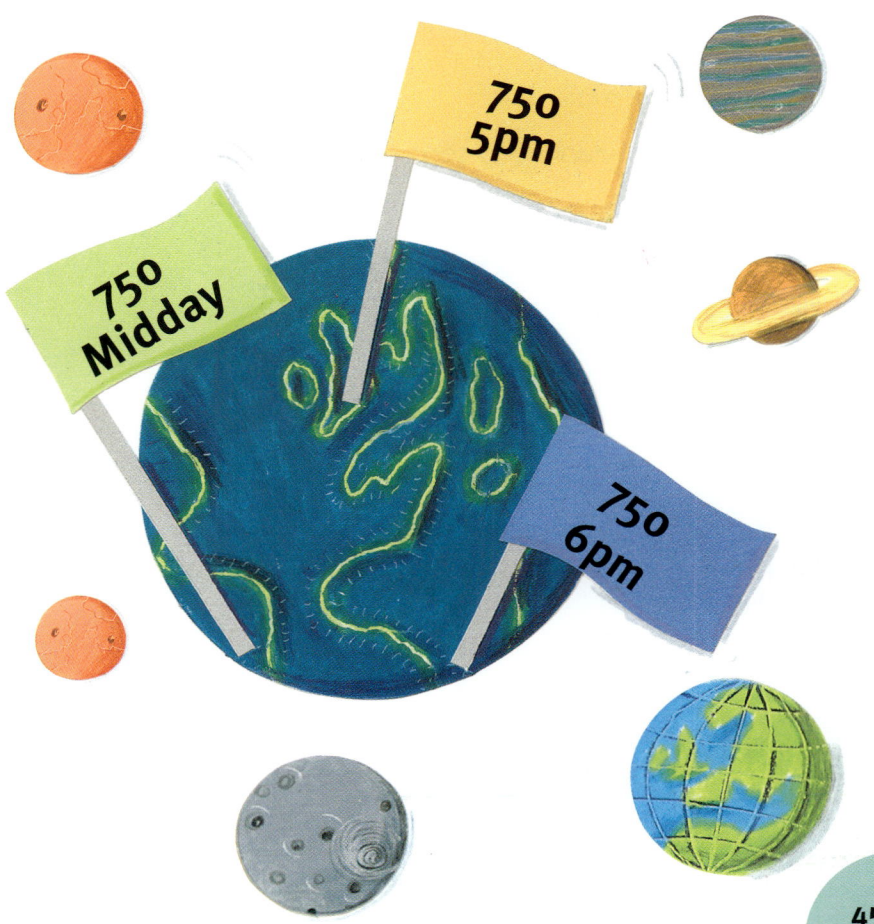

750 Midday

750 5pm

750 6pm

...OR PREFER TO WRITE?

E-mail – electronic mail – is a smart way of sending messages to other people who use the Internet and have e-mail accounts. If you want time to think about what you're saying rather than instant interactions, try e-mail.

LEARN TO...

- send an e-mail
- look at the reply and send an answer
- send a picture or a sound bite
- keep an address book
- find a pen pal

What is it?

E-mail is a bit like sending a letter, except it never has to be printed out and it gets where it's going in seconds. Instead of an address on an envelope, you have an e-mail address in a 'header' – a bit of information sent at the start of your message that tells the computers handling your message where it's going and who it's from.

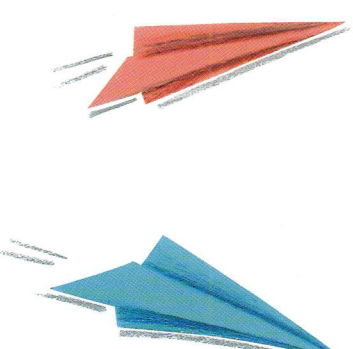

Getting an account

If you've got an ISP account, you've almost certainly got an e-mail account. And if not, you can easily get one. Even if you've already got an e-mail account set up with your ISP, you can start another one if you want to. This might be a good idea if you're not the only person using the computer. Then your e-mail won't get jumbled up with your mum's or your brother's.

It's easy to set up a web e-mail account, and you can then check your e-mail wherever you are – at home, at school, in the library, at a friend's house, in a cyber café – anywhere you can get on the Internet.

There are links from the Whizz Kids website to pages that let you set up a free e-mail account. Follow the instructions to start a new e-mail account – and don't forget the tips on page 8 about choosing a name and password.

Get writing

You need to know someone's e-mail address to send them a message. Start telling your friends your e-mail address so that they can mail you, and ask theirs so you can mail them.

Each e-mail message starts with:

- the e-mail address of the person you're sending it to.

- a little bit about the subject of your message (this helps people decide whether they need to read it immediately or whether to leave it till they've got more time).

If you're using a web page to send your e-mail, there will be spaces for the e-mail address, the subject and a big space for you to type your message.

HELP BOX

Make sure you type in addresses correctly – if you make any mistakes, the message won't get there.

So type what you want to say, and click the 'Send' button. E-mail messages travel by phone line and should go from one computer to another in a few seconds. Sometimes they get bogged down in slow computers and cables though, so don't assume the message you've sent will get there instantly.

If you want to save money on your phone bills, you can type your letter off-line first, and then cut and paste it into the e-mail page.

Smile!

A plain e-mail message can look a bit dull so smileys have been developed to help you show what you're feeling. The geeky word for smileys is 'emoticons' – icons that show your emotions. Here are some to try:

%-|	confused/dazed
:-=)	face with moustache
}:-(	frowning
:-)	happy
:-x	kissing
:@)	pig
:-(	sad
:-@	screaming
:-P	sticking tongue out
:-&	tongue-tied
;-)	winking
B-)	with shades

49

Save a stamp!

If you send a letter to more than one person, you need to use more than one stamp. If you send an e-mail, the same message is sent to as many people as you want at the same time – it costs the same (the price of the phone call) to send a message to one person as to a hundred! If you're sending the same info to lots of people – like party invitations – you can e-mail them all at once.

Here's how to send an e-mail to several people at once:

- Put all their e-mail addresses in the 'To' line of your e-mail. Put commas or semicolons between them, unless your e-mail site tells you to do something different.

```
Insert addresses from: Address Book   use commas between addresses
To:       luki@luki2000.co.uk, lauren@woppa2000.co.uk, alanb9@my
Subject:  come to a party!
Cc:                                     Bcc:
```

- If you're sending a message to one person and want someone else to see it, put the second person's address in the 'Cc' or 'Copy to' line.

```
Insert addresses from: Address Book   use commas between addresses
To:       luki@luki2000.co.uk
Subject:  Hear you got a new DVD...
Cc:       lauren@woppa2000.co.u    Bcc:
```

You've got mail

If you send someone an e-mail, they'll probably send you one back. If you're using a web e-mail service, you'll probably have to go to the website to look at your messages. There will be an 'inbox' or an option to 'Check mail'. Click on this to see if you've got any messages. Then click on a message or a 'View' button to open it and read it.

Instant reply

If you want to send an answer, look for a 'Reply' button. You won't need to type in the person's e-mail address, and the message may be copied in your reply for you to add bits.

Not only but also

You can send some extra bits and pieces along with your e-mail. These are called 'attachments' or 'enclosures' and can be other bits of work you've done on the computer.
For instance, you might want to send a picture you've made or a document you've written. You can e-mail your homework to your teacher like this!

Look for a button that lets you add an attachment or an enclosure. You'll then have to show the computer where on your hard disk the file is so that it sends the right one. It takes longer to send an e-mail with an attachment, especially if the attachment is a large file.

HELP BOX

Squashing files
If you download big files or want to send big files as attachments, you'll probably want to compress them (make them smaller) so that they go quicker. This is a bit like squashing a big thing into a small box. You need a bit of software to put it in and to unsquash it when you want to take it out. The Whizz Kids website has links to places you can download the most commonly-used compression software.

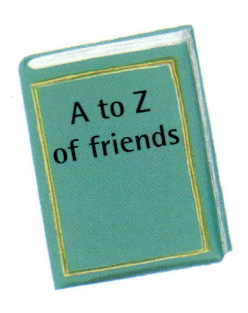

Check your address book

E-mail addresses aren't always easy to remember, but luckily you don't have to remember them! Look for an 'address book' option on the e-mail site. This lets you keep a note of the names and e-mail addresses you use most. Then, when you want to send a message, you just pick your friend's name from a list and their e-mail address will be pulled out for you.

Copy people's e-mail addresses into your address book as soon as you first use them or get an e-mail from them. It will save you typing in the address each time and save you the aggro of hunting for it when you've forgotten it.

Keep track

If you've got your computer set up so that the e-mail is copied directly on to your own computer, there's no limit to how much you can keep (until you run out of disk space!). But if you're using a web e-mail service where your e-mail is kept on someone else's computer and you look at it on-line, there will be a limit to how much you can keep.

Get into the habit of deleting messages you won't need again as soon as you have read them or replied to them. If you don't, your space will soon fill up and then other messages won't be able to get through.

HELP BOX

Bouncing messages

A message that can't get where it's going is 'bounced'. The person who sent it should get a message telling them their e-mail can't be delivered. It might bounce because the address is wrong or because the mailbox is full and can't take any more messages.

Got no mail?

Maybe your friends and relatives aren't on-line so you don't get any messages. Don't worry, you can get an e-mail pen pal to write to. It can be someone in your own country, or someone the other side of the world. It's cheaper and quicker than sending letters to a kid in a foreign country, and even more fun.

Look up the Whizz Kids website to find out how to track down an e-pen pal: **www.bigfishonline.co.uk/whizzkids**

SMART BROWSING

Now you can do whatever you want on the Web, it's time to learn how to tame your browser. You should be in charge!

LEARN TO...

- set the colours and text style used to display web pages
- look for things on a web page
- find pages you've used before
- get updates or plug-ins so your browser is always as cool as possible.

Colour changes

Some web pages set the colours used for links themselves, but others just let your browser pick the colour. If you don't change the settings, they will probably be:

- blue for links you haven't followed
- purple for links you have followed
- red when you move the pointer over a link (in Internet Explorer).

And, unless you choose something else, the background colour for the page will be grey and the ordinary (unlinked) text will be black. Pretty dreary, huh?

If you find these colours hard to read, or you just don't like them, you can change them.

Pick a colour...

If you're using Internet Explorer, open the 'Tools' or 'Edit' menu and choose 'Internet Options'. Use the 'General' tab and click on 'Colours'. Now you can click on the colour beside one of the options and choose a different colour.

If you're using Netscape, open the 'Edit' menu and choose 'Preferences'. Now click on 'Colours' in the category list on the left. (If you can't see 'Colours', click on the '+' or '▷' icon beside 'Appearance'.) And now click on the colour beside an option to change it.

> You can really jazz things up – but if you set bright orange text on a yellow background, it might be a bit hard to look at!

Font fun

While you're fiddling with the colours you can pick a different font, too. In Internet Explorer, there is a 'Font' button near the 'Colours' button. In Netscape it is another 'Appearance' category. Don't pick anything too wild or the pages will be really hard to read. You can also make the text bigger: in Internet Explorer, change the 'Text Size' from the 'View' menu. In Netscape, set the size when you choose the font.

Where are you?

You've done your search for 'African elephants' or whatever and you're at the start of a really long text page and can't see the bit you need. Now what? You don't have to read it all – you can get the browser to search the page for you. Open the 'Edit' menu and look for the 'Find' option. Now all you need to do is type in what you're looking for and tell the browser to start hunting.

HELP BOX

The browser will look for exactly what you type, so don't put 'stuff about elephants' because that phrase probably isn't on the page – just type 'elephant'.

Been there, done that

You've already found out (on page 30) how to add a page you like to your list of bookmarks or favorites. But what if you didn't mark the page and now you want to go back?

Your browser keeps a 'history' list. This is a list of all the pages you've looked at. You can look at the history and go back to anything you've seen in the last few days or even weeks. It's great if you've seen a site you like but can't remember how you got to it.

History explorer

If you're using Internet Explorer, there's a button labelled 'History' on the toolbar at the top. Click on it to show a list of places you've been (OK, it doesn't say you went to the loo or went to school today, but it shows where you've been on-line!).

It's probably got little icons for different days and weeks and you can click on these to see where you went on a particular day. If there's somewhere you recognize and you want to go to again, just follow the link.

In Netscape

If you're using Netscape, you have to try a bit harder. Open the 'Communicator' menu, and then look in the 'Tools' submenu for 'History'. Again, just click on a link to go back to a page you liked.

Manage your favorites

If you've got lots of favorites or bookmarks, it can be a hassle finding what you want. Smart surfers divide their favorites up into folders with sensible titles – it's much easier to manage. Use 'Organize Favorites' (from the 'Favorites' menu) if you're using Internet Explorer or 'Edit Bookmarks' from the Netscape 'Bookmarks' menu.

But don't get stuck
The people who write web browsers are working all the time to make them better so you can do more exciting things. To get the most from the Web, you need to keep your browser up to date. Do this by downloading the updates when they come out.

HELP BOX
Go to the web page for your browser to see if you have the latest version and download a newer one if you haven't. The urls are **www.microsoft.com** for Internet Explorer and **www.netscape.com** for Netscape.

Plug it in
Your browser can do quite a lot, but if you have some plug-ins it can do a whole lot more!

A plug-in is an extra bit of software that helps your browser out with the harder things you might want to do – like look at really fast animations and games, understand bits of programs on the Web and play movies or sound. There are links on the Whizz Kids website to some places to download the plug-ins you're most likely to need. They are free, so all you need to do is download them and follow the instructions to install them. If it isn't your computer, you should ask first, though.

What can it do?

With the right plug-ins you can do all the coolest stuff on the Web. You'll find there are more games you can do, little movies you can watch and cute programs to play with.

But it won't help you do your homework or clean your shoes!

Shockwave and flashes

Look for plug-ins to play Shockwave, Flash, Quicktime and Real Audio for starters. Then if you need anything else for a particular page, there will probably be a link to where you can download it.

Want a cookie?

A cookie is a little computer program that is stored on your computer and keeps a note of choices you've made on a particular website. If a web page uses cookies, it will download the cookie for you as long as your browser is prepared to take it. Then it will use the cookie to keep information – like your name so that it can show that on the page – or a note of options or games you've chosen in the past. It uses it to make the web page more personal. You can still use the page if you don't have the cookie, it just won't be quite as obviously 'yours'.

USEFUL WORDS

attachment
File that you send along with e-mail.

bookmark *see* **favorites.**

bounced
E-mail sent back to the sender because it can't be delivered.

browsing
Moving from one web page to another.

chat
Hold a 'conversation' with one or more friends in a chat group.

compress
Make a computer file take up less disk space.

cyberspace
The World Wide Web.

directory
Website with links to other sites arranged into categories.

download
Copy information or programs from a computer on the Internet on to your own computer.

e-mail
Electronic mail allows you to send messages over the Net to anyone else who has an e-mail address.

enclosure *see* **attachment.**

favorites
List of links to web pages that you have kept to return to later.

home page
The first page of a website or the page you have chosen to be displayed first whenever you start up your web browser.

hyperlink
A link to another document, usually a World Wide Web page. Clicking on the link opens the document.

icon
Little picture used to represent something, such as a document.

inbox
Folder that stores e-mail that you have received.

instant message
A text message you send to someone else's computer when you are both on-line.

Internet
Worldwide network of computers linked together.

Internet Service Provider (ISP)
Company that gives access to the Internet.

Internet time
Time system set up by Swatch which divides the day into 1,000 equal 'beats' and in which the time is the same all over the world.

link
Connection from one web page to another.

log in
Give a name and password so that you can use a computer, e-mail account, web page or program.

modem
Equipment that changes information your computer can understand into a form that can travel over the phone lines.

network
Group of computers connected together, usually by cabling. The Internet is an international network linked through the phone lines.

search engine
Computer program you use from a web page that searches the Internet for words or phrases you specify and finds websites and pages that contain them.

shareware
Computer programs that are provided free for you to try out, but for which you are expected to pay if you carry on using them.

smiley
Set of characters arranged to look like a face and used to get across feelings or attitudes.

surfing
Moving around the World Wide Web from one page to another.

upload
Copy information from your computer on to a computer on the Internet.

URL
Uniform Resource Locator: the address of a website or page.

wallpaper
Picture or pattern used as the background on your computer desktop.

web browser
Program that enables you to look at web pages on your computer.

webcam
Digital camera or digital video camera connected to the Internet that shows photos or videos.

website
A group of web pages linked together.

World Wide Web
The whole set of websites and pages available on the Internet.

INDEX

address books 46, 53
AOL 7
ask-an-expert sites 28
attachments 52, 62

back button 15
bookmarks 30, 58, 59, 62
books 38
bots 18
bounced 54, 62
browser windows 11, 12

cable TVs 6
cards 24, 27
CD-ROMs 6
chat 4, 40–44, 62
chat rooms 40–44
clip art 33, 34
colours 56–57
compressing files 52, 62
cookies 61

deleting 54
desktops 10, 37
directories 16, 17, 24, 27, 62
downloading 25, 32, 34, 35, 36, 37, 62

e-mail 4, 46–55, 62
e-mail accounts 47
e-mail addresses 8, 27, 48, 50–51, 53, 54
e-zines 30, 39

favorites *see* bookmarks
Flash 61
fonts 37, 57
free stuff 32

games 24, 25
gif files 34
Google 18

hard disk 32
Harry Potter 38, 39
history 58–59
home button 15
home pages 10, 12–13, 31, 62
homework 24, 27
Hubble Space Telescope 26

icons 10, 14, 37, 62
inbox 51, 62
instant messaging 44, 62
Internet Explorer 6, 11, 30, 31, 56, 57, 59, 60
Internet time 45, 63
Internet, the 4, 5, 6, 7, 9, 24, 40, 46, 47
ISPs 6, 11, 13, 39, 47, 62

jpeg files 34

links 9, 10, 14, 15, 16, 19, 21, 56, 59, 60, 63
log in 8, 63

Macs 5, 6, 11
modems 5, 6, 10, 33, 63
music 29

NASA 26
Netscape 6, 12, 30, 31, 57, 59, 60

passwords 4, 7, 8–9, 41
PCs 5, 6, 11
pen pals 55
phone lines 4, 5, 6, 7, 48
phone sockets 5, 10
pictures 33, 34
plug-ins 56, 60–61
puzzles 39

Quicktime 61

Real Audio 61

screensavers 37
search engines 16, 18–23, 24, 27, 63
searching a web page 56, 58
servers 14
shareware 36, 63
Shockwave 61
shortcuts 10, 11
smileys 49, 63
software 35, 36, 44, 60
sound 35
space 39
spiders 18

Teletubbies 39
text messages 4, 44

URLs 13, 24, 63

virus protection 37

wallpaper 37, 63
web browsers 6, 10, 11, 13, 56, 58, 60, 63
web radio 30
webcams 26, 63
webcasts 29
websites 12, 13, 16, 18, 21, 26, 27, 28, 32, 33, 63
Wilson, Jacqueline 38
Windows operating system 5
World Wide Web 4, 6, 13, 14, 18, 24, 25, 26, 27, 28, 29, 32, 33, 35, 38, 39, 60, 61, 62, 63

Yahoo 7
Yahooligans 17